Morning Glory Memory Keeper

A Record of Your Daily Routines & Life Stories

By Della Goldsworth

Table of Contents

Forward

In my work, I strive to give more than adequate care; I look for connection with my clients. I love connection with my clients. It keeps me motivated and keeps my clients and patients feeling respected as they deserve. But connection can be so difficult and frustrating when dementia, speech difficulties, or other barriers get in the way. Morning Glory Services will serve as a wonderful bridge of communication from the caregiver to the person receiving care. And while so many nurses and CNA's I've worked with have wished for it, it took Della to actually make Morning Glory Services happen. Della's energy and heart have created this wonderful tool to provide connection and dignity for you and your loved one.

I first met Della when we were both chasing our kids at a Waldorf school. We aren't close in age and appeared to have nothing much in common. But I have always been drawn to her energy. My background in palliative and hospice care would eventually bring Della and I together professionally when we met-up at the hospice I'm involved with and then we bonded more as she pursued her CNA training. I'm a massage therapist and CNA, and I do palliative and hospice body work in a variety of settings from private homes to Assisted Living and Skilled Nursing Facilities to our local Hospice Care Center. I have a trained focus in oncology massage and a passion for working with people with anxiety disorders. My background includes 20 years as a Doula, with a focus on pregnancy loss. Della's special talents involve working with people with dementia, organizing activities for the Skilled Nursing Facility where she works, directly caring for patients, along with her seemingly bottomless energy and compassion. Both of us share a desire to meet our patients and residents with respect, listen to their stories, hold the space needed and fill in when family may not be able.

I've watched Della's journey, heard her excitement about her residents and felt her frustration in wanting to connect deeper. Not everyone can do hospice work, and often people try it out, and find it's not for them. Della tried it out and the fit was so good she went to school to become a CNA, spent time working in a skilled nursing facility in several capacities, while developing this wonderful idea. But it's only as good as you make it. What you hold in your hands needs life breathed into it – the life of the loved one who takes her tea with cream and 2 spoons of sugar. The resident who likes his socks off at night, but on all day. The patient who studied language in college and would love to watch 1940's musicals and be read to in the evenings. The resident who may be wheelchair bound now, but as a young girl spent summers teaching dance and would like to listen to Leonard Cohen as much as possible. The dear loved one who had a small scoop of ice cream, after watching a MASH reruns, just before bed, for decades of her life. If we know these things, we can be ready with their socks unfolded, the film cued and the ice cream at the ready. That's called respect. And it's a dignity they have earned.

Julia Guderian LMT, CNA

To the residents in Life's Neighborhood at
Aegis Living of Redmond.
You are why this book was written.

For in the dew of little things
the heart finds its morning and is refreshed.
-Khalil Gibran

Introduction

One of the most important elements of caregivers is the connection we have with our patients. During their time with us, we are involved in the most intimate parts of their day. We can maintain our patients' dignity by treating them as individuals, by connecting with each of them in ways that are unique to them, and caring for them based on their individual preferences.

After spending time with people who have Alzheimer's and other forms of dementia, I found them to be interesting, amazing individuals whom I wanted to get to know better. However, it was hard to find out the details I wanted to know to really connect with the people I was caring for. One of my residents once enthusiastically told me about a trip to Jerusalem she took when she was very young. Her favorite part of that trip had been riding a camel. She became frustrated when she couldn't remember more. I wish I could have just an hour or two to talk with their previous selves, to find out all these stories. Knowing their stories enables caregivers to connect with their residents on a deeper level.

A few reasons you need this workbook:
- You or a family member has been diagnosed with Alzheimer's or another form of dementia.
- You or a family member has had a stroke, been in an accident, or diagnosed with MS, ALS, or any other disease that limits your ability to effectively communicate.
- You are healthy now and want possible future caregivers to know necessary information about you.

No one wants to imagine that we, or someone we love, will not be able to communicate with those around us. We might be intimidated by the thought of developing a form of dementia, having a stroke, or getting diseases that limit physical or mental capacity. It could be uncomfortable to admit that it may happen to us. It's heartbreaking when it happens to someone we love.

Morning Glory Memory Keeper is here to help.

How to Use the Morning Glory Memory Keeper

There are two main parts in this workbook. In the first, you'll be recording your personal preferences and daily habits and routines. The second will go into detail about your favorite memories.

Most people find that there are too many questions to be answered in one sitting. If you get tired or upset, take a break. Enjoy working through the book at your own pace.

If you're filling this out for someone else, have them with you if possible. They might share details you are unaware of.

At the beginning of each section, there are suggestions and examples to get you started. If a section or suggestion doesn't speak to you or doesn't seem relevant, skip it. The routines you write down will be those that help bring normality and grounding to your days. The memory stories will be those that bring a smile to your face.

Write down memories that come to mind first, the ones that make you happy just to think of them. The details you include might seem silly or inconsequential. Include them anyway. For example: "In high school, on my birthday, me and couple of my friends decided to go climb the water tower. I'd done it before, and wanted to show the new guy how it was done. We got all the way to the top, and I fell. I'd climbed it the most of all of us, but I fell. What was amazing was that I only got a scratch on my pinky finger from catching myself on the way down. Talk about adrenalin! Of course, I climbed right back up, since both my friends were laughing at me." Make the memory real for you. How old were you, who was with you, what happened. Having these details will make the memory feel exceptionally, uniquely, yours.

- Leave parts blank or cross them out if they aren't relevant.
- Choose answers that are strong, things you love or hate, not things that would fall into the "this is okay, I guess" category.
- Include details that "paint the picture" clearly for those reading it later.

Daily Life

In this section, we'll talk about who you are today. What you like, don't like, and how you like to spend your day. We'll go into how you like your environment to be, how you like to look, and what you like to eat. Short answers are fine here, but go into detail if you want to.

The Basics

What is your full name?

....

What do you like to be called?

....

When is your birthday?

....

Where were you born?

....

Where did you grow up?

....

....

....

....

Where do you live now?

....

....

....

Are you married/in a relationship? With whom?

....

....

....

Do you have kids? What are their names?

....

....

....

....

....

Do you have grandkids? Names?

....

....

Great-Grandkids? Names?

....

....

....

....

What are your close friends' names and how long have you known them?

....

....

....

....

....

....

....

....

....

....

....

Routines

Habits

Do you drink coffee or tea? If so, how do you take it?

....

....

....

Do you smoke (cigarettes, vaping, etc.)?

....

....

Do you drink alcohol? What kind and when?

....

....

Do you take showers or baths? Hot, warm, or cool?

....

....

Do you like to shower in the morning or at night?

....

....

Morning

What time do you get up?

....

....

....

What does your morning routine look like?

....

....

....

....

....

....

....

....

....

....

....

What do you like to do after breakfast (if you have a day with no plans)?

....

....

....

....

....

....

....

....

Anything else important to know about your mornings?

....

....

....

....

....

....

....

....

Evening

What time do you go bed?

....

....

....

What does your routine look like before bed?

....

....

....

....

....

....

....

....

....

....

....

What do you like to do before bed (read, watch TV, etc)?

....

....

....

....

....

....

....

What do you wear to bed? Pajamas? Nightgown? Socks?

Nothing?

....

....

....

....

....

What bedcovers do you like (a single sheet, one blanket,

several blankets)?

....

....

Do you tuck in the sheets?

....

....

....

How many pillows do you like? Soft? Firm?

....

....

....

Do you like to sleep with a fan on or the window open?

....

....

....

Do you like to sleep in a cold room or a warm one?

....

....

....

Do you like a light in your room or the room to be very dark?

....

....

Anything else important to know about your evening?

....

....

....

....

....

....

....

....

....

....

....

....

....

....

....

....

Food & Drink

What do you like to eat and drink for breakfast?

....

....

....

....

....

....

....

....

What do you like to eat and drink for lunch?

....

....

....

....

....

....

....

What do you like to eat and drink for dinner?

....

....

....

....

....

....

What are your favorite snacks?

....

....

....

....

....

What are your favorite things to drink?

....

....

....

....

....

Do you drink alcohol? Do you avoid it?

What are your favorites?

....

....

....

....

....

....

....

What are your favorite desserts?

....

....

....

....

....

....

....

....

What are your comfort foods when you are sad?

....

....

....

....

....

....

What do you eat when you are celebrating?

....

....

....

....

....

....

What foods/drinks do you dislike?

....

....

....

....

....

....

....

....

....

....

....

....

Any other favorite foods not mentioned above?

....

....

....

....

....

....

....

....

....

Interests

Entertainment

Do you enjoy watching TV or movies?

....

....

....

....

....

....

What genres do you like best (comedy, drama, action, noir,

classics, etc.)?

....

....

....

....

....

....

What genres do you dislike?

....

....

....

What are your favorite TV shows/channels?

....

....

....

....

....

....

....

....

....

....

....

....

What are your favorite movies?

....

....

....

....

....

....

....

....

....

Who are your favorite actors/performers?

....

....

....

....

....

....

....

....

Do you enjoy reading? What (books, magazines, etc.)?

....

....

....

....

....

....

....

....

Which genres?

....

....

....

....

....

....

....

Who are your favorite authors?

....

....

....

....

....

....

....

....

Hobbies

What are your hobbies? Use the below list for inspiration, but it's far from a complete list.

- Drawing/painting/sculpture (favorite artists?)
- Technology
- Knitting/crocheting
- Sewing/weaving
- Video games/console games/board games
- Collecting (what and why?)
- Automotive
- Hunting/fishing
- Hiking
- Gardening

Activities

How active are you?

....

....

....

....

....

....

....

What indoor activities/exercises do you enjoy?

....

....

....

....

....

....

....

What outdoor activities/exercises do you enjoy?

....

....

....

....

....

....

....

....

....

Do you prefer solitary or group activities?

....

....

....

....

....

....

....

....

Do you play games (dice, cards, board, video)?

....

....

....

....

....

....

....

....

Do you like to go for walks? Long or short? What do you like to do while walking?

....

....

....

....

....

....

Music

Do you enjoy music?

....

....

....

What genres do you enjoy (Country, Jazz, Blues, Rock, Funk, Soul, Classical, Pop, Gospel, Ska, Rap, Reggae, Techno, Hip Hop, Punk, Grunge, Indie, Opera, Religious, Swing, Choral, Folk, Bluegrass, Acapella, Rockabilly, Showtunes, etc.)?

....

....

....

....

....

....

....

....

....

Who are your favorite artists/bands?

....

....

....

....

....

....

....

....

Favorite albums?

....

....

....

....

....

....

....

....

How do you like to listen to music (radio, cassette, CD, MP3 player, etc.)?

....

....

....

Do you play an instrument?

....

....

....

....

....

Did you ever play in a band? Did you enjoy it?

....

....

....

....

....

What kind of music did you like as a teenager?

....

....

....

....

....

Would you rather listen to fast, upbeat music, or slow, calm

music?

....

....

....

....

....

When do you prefer music and when you prefer silence?

....

....

....

....

....

Do you and your partner have a special song?

....

....

....

Do you like to attend concerts?

 Favorite ones you have been to?

....

....

....

....

....

....

Music makes me feel...

....

....

....

....

....

Environment

Bedroom

How do you like your room to look?

....

....

....

....

....

....

What do you like to have in your room?

....

....

....

....

....

....

....

What do you like to have on your bedside table?

....

....

....

....

....

....

Do you prefer your blinds and curtains open or closed?

....

....

....

Do you like to have a TV in your room?

....

....

....

Do you sit in bed or in a chair to watch TV?

....

....

....

Do you prefer your clothing hung up or in drawers?

....

....

....

....

....

....

List five things you would like to have in your bedroom (for example, fresh flowers, your favorite photo of your family, military awards, your journal or a notebook, slippers, etc.):

1. ....

2. ....

3. ....

4. ....

5. ....

Bathroom

What products do you like on your counter?

....

....

....

....

....

....

What products do you use in your shower?

....

....

....

....

....

Do you use an electric shaver or a razor?

....

....

....

What do you use for shaving cream?

....

....

....

Do you prefer to facial hair or to be clean shaven?

....

....

....

Anything else you like to have in your bathroom?

....

....

....

....

....

....

....

....

....

Public Areas

Do you prefer to sit by yourself or in groups?

....

....

....

Do you like sunny days or cloudy ones? Rain? Thunder

storms?

....

....

....

Do you like to sit outside? In the sun or in shade?

....

....

....

....

Do you prefer to dine alone or with people?

....

....

....

Personal Appearance

What do you like to wear during a relaxing day?

....

....

....

....

....

Do you prefer shoes or sandals? Do you wear shoes indoors?

....

....

....

....

How do you like to wear your hair?

....

....

....

....

....

Do you use hair products? Which ones?

....

....

....

....

....

....

Do you wear makeup? What? Preferred brands?

....

....

....

....

....

....

Do you use facial or body lotion?

....

....

....

....

What scents do you prefer for personal hygiene products?

....

....

....

....

....

....

Do you like polish on your fingernails? What colors? Do you
like your nails long or short?

....

....

....

....

....

Anything else important to know about how you like to look?

....

....

....

....

Holidays

Birthday

How do you celebrate your birthday?

....

....

....

....

Do you have a special meal you like to eat?

....

....

....

....

What dessert do you eat (cake, pie, other)? What kind (be

specific)?

....

....

....

....

Other Holidays

Which holidays are important to you?

....

....

....

....

....

....

....

....

....

How do you celebrate them?

....

....

....

....

....

....

Religion

Do you consider yourself religious/spiritual/agnostic/atheist/anti-religion?

....

....

How important is your religion/belief to you?

....

....

....

....

What beliefs/practices are important to you?

....

....

....

....

....

....

What traditions or rituals are important for you to continue?

45

....

....

....

....

....

....

....

....

Which religious holidays do you observe? In what ways?

....

....

....

....

....

....

....

....

Are you okay with participating in/observing events of other religions (for example, singing or listening to Christmas songs if you're Jewish)?

....

....

....

....

....

....

Is there anything else important to know about your religious practices?

....

....

....

....

....

....

....

Other Important Details

Imagine yourself in a place where you couldn't communicate well with the people taking care of you. Is there anything we haven't covered that you'd like them to know? Idiosyncrasies, habits, beliefs, likes, dislikes, etc.

....

....

....

....

....

....

....

....

....

....

....

....

....

....

Your History

This is for your personal stories. Include when, where, with who, what, and why. Add those little details that bring the story to life for you. It's okay if the story isn't linear, or strays from the original prompt. Not all sections need answers. This is the place for those stories that bring you the most happiness and make you smile.

Family Tree

Let's start with a family tree. Name parents, grandparents, siblings, children, grandchildren, great-grandchildren.

....

....

....

....

....

....

....

....

....

....

Family Stories

Are there any family stories that you love from before you were born?

....

....

....

....

....

....

....

....

....

....

....

Where is your family from?

....

....

....

....

Childhood

Think back to early childhood, from as young as you can remember to your teen years.

Example Story: "My mother's name was Marcelle, she was 24 when I was born. We lived way up in the mountains, in a cabin with no heat and no indoor bathroom. I still remember how cold it got in the winter! But my mother would wrap me in my grandmother's quilt - I still have that today – and we'd get toasty warm by the fire. When I was four, we moved into town. I loved having heat in the house, but I sometimes missed that time wrapped in that quilt with my mom."

PROMPTS

Parent's occupations

Childhood homes

Stories with siblings

Elementary, Middle, or High School stories

Family pets

Summer vacations

....

....

....

....

....

....

....

....

Adulthood

PROMPTS

College/
University

Military life

Friends

Think back on your adult life.
College, working, relationships.
Choose a few favorite memories and
go into detail. Who were you with?
When was it? Where? Why were you
there? What did you do?

For example, "Jim and I moved to
Texas after we were married to live near his parents. I didn't
like his dad very much, but his mother was very welcoming,
and even taught me how to make his favorite carrot cake. He
didn't like the kind with pineapple, so she showed me how
she used applesauce instead. We lived in a tiny house, which
became even tinier when we had our first baby, Nancy. We
moved to a bigger house in Austin when Nancy was 3 and
our son Rick was born. I loved that house because the
backyard was huge! Rick built a fort in one of the trees, but it
came down in a storm when he was a teenager."

These stories can be linear, focused on one event or person,
or they can meander, as your mind moves from one part of
the memory to another. Whichever way your mind brings up
the past, write it that way. And remember, write the
memories that make you smile. Prompts will be suggested
along the way.

....

....

....

....

....

....

....

....

....

....

PROMPTS

Dating

Partner/spouse

....

....

....

....

....

....

....

....

....

....

....

....

....

....

....

....

....

....

....

PROMPTS

First job

Favorite job

Volunteer work

....

....

....

....

....

....

....

....

....

....

....

....

....

....

What stood out to you as the highlight of the vacation might not mean anything to anyone else, but if it was your favorite part, write it. If eating breakfast at the little café down the street from your hotel in Paris was more special than seeing the Eiffel Tower, talk about that.

PROMPTS

Travel

Road Trips

Favorite Vacations

....

....

....

....

....

....

....

....

....

....

....

....

....

Think back through the different stages. Your favorite memory doesn't have to be a big event. If when you think of our daughter, you remember the time she snuck an orange to eat in her bath, write about that. Include the details that make it real for you. The song you sang to her while she bathed, how she hid the peel in her towel, how she would only use the shampoo in the yellow bottle, or how she was scared of bubble baths.

PROMPTS

Children

Grandchildren

Great-Grandchildren

....

....

....

....

....

....

....

....

....

....

....

....

PROMPTS

Animals

Pets

....

....

....

....

....

....

....

....

....

....

....

....

....

....

....

....

....

....

....

PROMPTS

Famous people you met

Events you took part in

....

....

....

....

....

....

....

....

....

....

....

....

....

....

....

....

....

....

PROMPTS

Life goals you've accomplished

Life lessons learned

....

....

....

....

....

....

....

....

....

....

....

....

....

....

....

....

....

....

....

....

....

....

....

....

....

....

....

....

....

....

....

Other Important Memories

Are there other important stories of your life not recorded above? Use the next few pages to write down happy memories that either don't fit in the listed categories, or come to mind after those pages are filled.

....

....

....

....

....

....

....

....

....

....

....

....

....

....

Last Steps

- Keep a copy with your will.
- Give a copy to the person who has power of attorney in the event you are unable to advocate for yourself. Tell them you want a copy to be given to anyone giving you care, and used in your Care Plan.
- Talk to your family members about the Memory Keeper, and how to use it on your behalf if necessary.
- Give a copy to any friends or family members you feel are appropriate.
- If you are filling this workbook out for someone currently in a care facility or using in-home care, give a copy to the caregiver and/or head nurse. Let the care staff know you would like the information in it to be used in daily care.
- Update the Memory Keeper when necessary.

To join our online community, ask questions, watch how-to videos, and learn about future projects, join our Facebook page at
www.facebook.com/morningglorymemorykeeper/

For bulk orders, questions, or to give feedback, please email: info@morninggloryservices.com.
We promise not to sell your personal info.
Thank you!

Acknowledgements

I can't even begin to impart to you how true it is that without the help from so many people this book would never have been written, much less published.

First, always, Jim, who despite knowing how I can jump into new things without any thought to their practicality, supported me 100% in this endeavor. He is my anchor, and the reason I can follow my dreams with near abandon. He also contributed huge amounts to the editing process. Thank you, my love. You da bestest.

This book would have stayed a small little side project without the help of my publishing coach, Tajuana Ross. She pushed me, and continues to push me, far past my comfort zone and into possibilities that blind me with their awesomeness.

For introducing me to Tajuana, and always being there to tell me I rock (even when I feel like I'm in way over my head), thank you Danielle!

Must give huge thanks to all the people in my world who listened to my crazy idea (after listening to a thousand of my crazy ideas) and without hesitation said, "Yes! You can do this!" I know I'll leave out important ones, so please forgive me if you don't see your name, but here goes...Audrey, Natasha, Erin. Emily – for your support and proofreading, thank you! Tammy, thank you for a wonderful Author page.

Sharon, you know you get your own line, woman. Here's to Wednesday nights. Here's to cutting out the unnecessary. Here's to you. Love you!

Mom, Dad, Mick, and Kate. I am so happy to have been raised by and with you Nuts. I am who I am because of you.

To those who've been in my life for so long you are like sisters, there for me at any hour: Andrea, Tania, (and Kathy-babe, I miss you every day), I love you, always will. Thank you for everything you are.

To Julia G., who said, "Be a Hospice volunteer!", a simple statement that changed my life path forever. She and her sister Jennifer also gave me invaluable editing advice for which I am so grateful.

Thank you, Meg Harmon, Music Therapist, for her contribution to the musical section.

Thank you to Lisa Marien, for her absolutely beautiful graphic design and cover work.

Kaia (my wonderful aspiring editor, who caught four errors no-one else did!), Ben, and Jasmine.
You are the sunshine in my world.
I'm beyond happy to be your mom and step-mom.
All three of you make me so proud!
I know you will continue to show me on the daily
that "normal" is boring!
I LOVE YOU BIG TIME.

Photo by Hildebrand Photography

About the Author

Della Goldsworth's passion for becoming an advocate for people with dementia began with volunteer work in hospice care. She noticed that the little things, such as knowing a resident's favorite memories or how they liked their tea, added to their quality of life. This passion grew into an idea for a guide to help caregivers maintain their residents' dignity and make life with dementia or a communication-limiting disease as comfortable and fulfilling as possible.

When Della isn't caring for the elderly, she devotes her time to her partner, three kids, various cats, dogs, chickens, and the occasional foster duck egg. She does it all by self-care, living a healthy life style of eating whole foods (most of the time), exercise, and baking all the cakes.

She's an approachable person and wants everyone to know she has arms always ready to give a hug.

The Morning Glory Memory Keeper is her first foray into writing.

Made in the USA
Lexington, KY
07 May 2017